W9-AVC-396

UNDERSTANDING THE PARANORMAL

INVESTIGATING UFOs and ALIENS

THERESE SHEA

Britannica®
Educational Publishing

IN ASSOCIATION WITH

ROSEN
EDUCATIONAL SERVICES

Published in 2015 by Britannica Educational Publishing (a trademark of Encyclopædia Britannica, Inc.) in association with The Rosen Publishing Group, Inc.
29 East 21st Street, New York, NY 10010

Distributed exclusively by Rosen Publishing.
To see additional Britannica Educational Publishing titles, go to rosenpublishing.com.

First Edition

Britannica Educational Publishing
J.E. Luebering: Director, Core Reference Group
Anthony L. Green: Editor, Compton's by Britannica

Rosen Publishing
Hope Lourie Killcoyne: Executive Editor
Shalini Saxena: Editor
Nelson Sá: Art Director
Brian Garvey: Designer
Cindy Reiman: Photography Manager

Library of Congress Cataloging-in-Publication Data

Shea, Therese, author.
Investigating UFOs and aliens/Therese Shea.—First edition.
     pages cm.—(Understanding the paranormal)
Includes bibliographical references and index.
ISBN 978-1-62275-849-4 (library bound)—ISBN 978-1-62275-850-0 (paperback)—
ISBN 978-1-62275-851-7 (6-pack)
1. Unidentified flying objects—Juvenile literature. 2. Human-alien encounters—Juvenile literature. I. Title.
TL789.2.S53 2015
001.942—dc23

2014021040

Manufactured in the United States of America

Photo credits: Cover, p. 1 Photobank gallery/Shutterstock.com; pp. 4–5 Albert Ziganshin/Shutterstock.com; p. 6 National Radio Astronomy Observatory; p. 8 Rex Features via AP Images; p. 10 NASA/JPL/University of Arizona; p. 11 Science & Society Picture Library/Getty Images; p. 12 Apic/Hulton Archive/Getty Images; pp. 15, 36 Science Source; p. 16 Encyclopædia Britannica, Inc.; p. 17 © Patrice Marty/Fotolia; pp. 18–19 AFP/Getty Images; p. 21 Joe Raedle/Hulton Archive/Getty Images; p. 22 Barry King/WireImage/Getty Images; p. 25 National Institute of Standards and Technology; p. 27 Popperfoto/Getty Images; p. 29 © AP Images; p. 30 Science Source/Photo Researchers/Getty Images; p. 31 SPL/Science Source; p. 34 Mary Evans/Ronald Grant/Everett Collection; p. 37 © Universal Pictures/courtesy Everett Collection; p. 39 © Lucasfilm/Entertainment Pictures/ZUMAPRESS.com; p. 40 Ralph Crane/The LIFE Picture Collection/Getty Images; interior pages background images © iStockphoto.com/Kivilvim Pinar, © iStockphoto.com/mitja2.

CONTENTS

INTRODUCTION

I n April 2014, four people in Orlando, Florida, saw an object with red and green lights streak downward across the night sky. It passed behind a building, soared upward again, stopped in midair, and then turned. One of the witnesses was a pilot who claimed that no man-made aircraft could move like that at the speeds observed. What did these people see? A trick of the light? A classified government aircraft? An actual alien spacecraft?

Many people have reported seeing unusual objects like this in the sky. Whether life exists on other planets or not, the idea of unidentified flying objects (UFOs) and aliens has long excited and fascinated people on Earth. The presence of aliens on or beyond our planet has never been proven, but some people continue to believe in, look for signs of, and listen to stories about encounters with alien life.

Why are people so interested in alien life? Perhaps it is because now that we know how huge the universe really is, it seems possible that Earth is not the only life-supporting planet. Even among the often skeptical scientific community, there are some advocates for keeping an open mind about extraterrestrial life.

Aliens are often depicted like this, with large heads and eyes shaped like almonds. This most likely comes from literature on alien life.

CHAPTER ONE

WHAT IS AN ALIEN?

The word "alien" is a popular word for an extra-terrestrial life-form, or a being that originated beyond Earth. No one knows if extraterrestrial life exists or ever existed, but some scientists think that it is possible. The branch of biology concerned with extra-terrestrial life—from microscopic organisms to intelligent beings—is called exobiology or astrobiology. Scientists in this field consider the conditions necessary for life, how it evolves, how to detect alien life-forms, and the environments in

which they might live, whether in our own solar system or on any of the numerous planets orbiting other stars.

EXTRATERRESTRIAL LIFE

The precise requirements for life are not known. All living things on Earth are based on the element carbon and need water for chemical reactions. Hydrogen, nitrogen, phosphorous, sulfur, oxygen, and other elements are also essential. However, if alien life-forms exist, they might be very different from any living thing on Earth. Such life-forms might be difficult to detect or even recognize as life.

At a basic level, living things must be made of atoms that bond to form a variety of molecules at the temperatures in their environment. They probably require a liquid (water or perhaps ammonia, hydrogen cyanide, or liquid hydrocarbons) for chemical reactions. The environment would have this liquid at or near the surface. Life-forms would also need sunlight or another energy source, protection from ultraviolet radiation, and probably an atmosphere.

Extraterrestrial intelligence is one step further than extraterrestrial life. It means life from another world that is capable of thinking and working toward a

Radio telescopes like this one in Virginia are capable of seeking out extraterrestrial signals from deep within outer space. However, nothing has been detected yet.

MOVE OVER LITTLE GREEN MEN

Many people's concept of alien life is that of little green or gray beings with large heads and huge eyes. These ideas

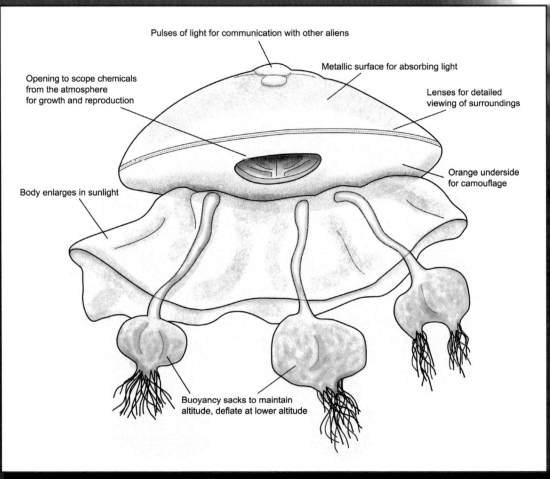

Pulses of light for communication with other aliens

Metallic surface for absorbing light

Opening to scope chemicals from the atmosphere for growth and reproduction

Lenses for detailed viewing of surroundings

Body enlarges in sunlight

Orange underside for camouflage

Buoyancy sacks to maintain altitude, deflate at lower altitude

Just as Earth has life-forms that have adapted to their differing environments in different ways, alien life-forms might have features that are better suited to different surroundings.

come from books and films, and these aliens resemble life-forms we know well—people. At least one scientist suggests that people are imagining extraterrestrial intelligence all wrong.

Dr. Maggie Aderin-Pocock envisioned one way alien life could have adapted to a planet similar to Jupiter. She hypothesized that silicon-based aliens could look somewhat like floating jellyfish and survive on sunlight and chemicals. They might not necessarily be intelligent enough to make contact with Earth, though. Aderin-Pocock also reminds people that aliens on other worlds might have previously existed but became extinct before human life evolved.

purpose. Work in the field of astrobiology has provided some evidence that evolution of other intelligent species in the Milky Way Galaxy is not impossible.

EXPLORATIONS

Space exploration has been an important part of the search for extraterrestrial life. Unmanned probes have visited every planet in the solar system, plus many moons, asteroids, and comets. Places in the solar system that seem most likely to

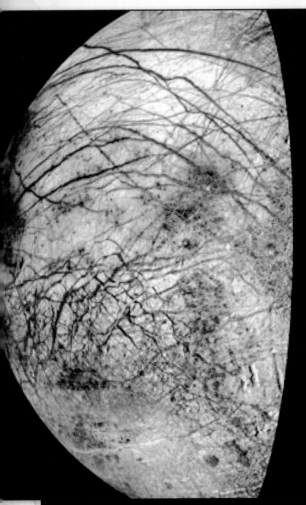

Jupiter's moon Europa, shown here, has a surface mostly composed of water ice and most likely salty minerals. However, liquid water is thought to lie below the surface.

have harbored life—most likely microbes—now or in the past, include Mars, Jupiter's moon Europa, and Saturn's moon Enceladus. All three have, or once had, liquid water at or near the surface. Saturn's moon Titan, which appears to have lakes of liquid methane, is also of great interest.

Since the 1990s, astronomers have detected and studied exoplanets, or planets outside the solar system. In fact, more than 1,700 exoplanets have been confirmed. These efforts suggest that there could be many worlds on which life, or even intelligent life, might arise. Whether this life has already arrived on Earth in UFOs is a different matter.

PROBING FOR EXTRATERRESTRIAL LIFE

The National Aeronautics and Space Administration (NASA) has sent probes to the farthest reaches of our solar system and equipped them with messages—just in case of contact with alien life. The *Pioneer 10* and *Pioneer 11* probes, launched in 1972–73, each carry a plaque that depicts a man and a woman, our solar system, and the location of Earth and the sun.

The twin *Voyager* probes sent in 1977 to explore the outer solar system carry images and sounds of different cultures on Earth, music from various cultures and time periods, and greetings in fifty-five languages.

A scientist mounts a gold-plated record of sounds of Earth onto the Voyager 2 *spacecraft, launched in 1977 and now beyond our solar system.*

This is what the U-2 spy plane looked like in 1957. It was much faster and higher flying than other airplanes of that time, sparking UFO rumors.

WHAT IS A UFO?

When many people think of a UFO, they think of an alien's spaceship. Actually, UFO is an abbreviation for the phrase "unidentified flying object." In other words, any object moving in the sky that is not recognizable is a UFO. That does not necessarily mean that the object is from another world. The unidentified object might have been a natural astronomical object, such as a star, bright planet, or meteor, that the witness did not recognize. Many other UFOs have turned out to be weather balloons, hot gases, birds, or simply a trick of the light. Often these sightings happened under unusual weather conditions.

UFOs have also included man-made aircraft, especially new types of military craft being kept secret by a government. Among them have been top-secret spy planes that the U.S. government did not want the public to know about. The Central Intelligence Agency (CIA) estimates that more than one-half of the UFOs reported from the late 1950s through the 1960s were U-2 and SR-71 Blackbird spy planes. At the time, the government did not reveal what they were. The RQ-3 Darkstar and B-2 Spirit are two other U.S. military planes with unusual shapes that could cause a spike in UFO reports.

Could UFOs of today be other classified aircraft that the public does not know about? Even if some of them are, it could not explain all sightings. UFO history goes back to ancient times, before the beginnings of aviation. (As we have already seen, however, UFOs can also be attributed to a variety of natural phenomena.)

CHAPTER TWO

UFO HISTORY

Almost every civilization with a written history has recorded sightings of strange shapes and lights in the skies. The first known account appears in the Bible and may date back to 592 BCE. In the Book of Ezekiel, the prophet called Ezekiel sees objects in the sky shaped like spinning, sparkling wheels with creatures within them. Some people think Ezekiel was encountering ancient alien astronauts in UFOs.

In the 800s CE, a French archbishop described his community's belief in ships that came from above the clouds. Beings that were said to have fallen from these floating vessels were stoned to death.

One of the first well-documented UFO sightings occurred in 1561 in Nuremberg, Germany. A newspaper published that year describes red, blue, and black balls or plates, crosses, and tubes that appeared to battle each

This is an artist's depiction of the 1561 events at Nuremberg, Germany. The strange colorful objects that "battled" each other above the city were many shapes and sizes, witnesses said.

other in the sky over the city. However, UFO mania did not really begin until the mid-twentieth century, with the first sighting of a "flying saucer."

ENTER THE FLYING SAUCER

The term "flying saucer" was coined in 1947—accidently. A businessman named Kenneth Arnold told reporters

The Flying Saucer as I Saw it... by Kenneth Arnold
Per copy 60¢

Kenneth Arnold wrote a book (published in 1950) about what he saw near Mount Rainier. This is an autographed cover.

that, while flying a private airplane near Mount Rainier in Washington State, he spotted nine objects cruising in formation at a speed of more than 1,600 miles (2,500 kilometers) per hour. Arnold described the objects as moving like "a saucer skipping across the water." After that first report, Arnold's description was shortened, and it soon became popular to call all UFOs flying saucers.

From time to time in 1947, people in various parts of the United States and some other countries reported seeing strange objects in the sky and

CROP CIRCLES

Some people have pointed to crop circles, or large geometric patterns of flattened crops, as evidence of UFO landings. Beginning in the late 1970s, simple crop circles began to appear regularly in southern England. Over the years, they became more complex. Certain people who studied crop circles were convinced that their intricacy and the fact that the plants were bent but not broken meant that they could not have been produced by humans. However, in 1991, two men confessed to having made more than two hundred crop circles with ropes and boards.

This is a crop circle in a British field. The elaborate design looks as though an advanced spaceship might have landed here.

claimed that they were spacecraft piloted by aliens. In the midst of this "flying saucer" craze, unusual material fell to the ground about July 4 near Roswell, New Mexico.

WHAT HAPPENED AT ROSWELL?

On July 8, an eager young officer at the Roswell Army Air Field (RAAF) issued an extraordinary and unauthorized press release. He circulated the story that a "flying disk" had been retrieved from a local ranch. The *Roswell Daily Record* immediately picked up the press release and printed the account with the headline "RAAF Captures Flying Saucer on Ranch in Roswell Region."

The young officer was reprimanded, and the base released information stating that the "saucer" had actually been a weather balloon, or rather a cluster of balloons, carrying a radar target made of foiled paper fastened to a wooden frame. The *Fort Worth Star-Telegram* published a photograph of two amused air force officers posing with the debris, which consisted of some flexible, silvery material. The *Roswell Daily Record* also carried the correction and featured an interview with the rancher, William (Mac) Brazel. Brazel, however, did not believe that the debris he discovered was from a weather balloon.

CONSPIRACY!

The Roswell Incident, as it came to be called, served as the basis for many hoaxes and conspiracy theories. In 1950, the book *Behind the Flying Saucers* was published. It alleged that the U.S. government possessed at least three alien space-ships, along with the bodies of their occupants. An investigation revealed that the author, Frank Scully, was told the story by two men who were selling an oil-locating device they claimed was based on alien technology.

In 1980, another book, *The Roswell Incident*, came out. The

Major Jesse Marcel from the Roswell Army Air Field holds the debris found on Brazel's ranch in Roswell, New Mexico, in 1947. The debris was shown to be of human origin.

book's coauthors, Charles Berlitz and William L. Moore, labeled the weather balloon explanation a "cover story." They argued that the original debris, which they believed was from a crashed flying saucer, had been flown to Wright Field near Dayton, Ohio, and material from a weather balloon was "hastily substituted." Berlitz and Moore cited the recollections of former Roswell staff officer Major Jesse Marcel. He and Brazel's son described materials that were supposedly quite technologically advanced.

Berlitz and Moore were correct about one thing: the government's claim that a weather balloon crashed at Roswell was untrue. In 1994, the U.S. Air Force admitted that the recovered material was actually from a U.S. spy balloon. It was an attempt to monitor anticipated nuclear tests by the Soviet Union.

Other Roswell hoaxes include the "MJ-12 documents" of 1984, which purported to show that a secret operation was launched by President Harry Truman to handle the Roswell Incident, and a fake alien autopsy film from 1995, which supposedly shows the dissection of an alien corpse. Such deceptions helped make the term "Roswell Incident" famous.

WHAT IS AREA 51?

For many years, Area 51 was so secret that the U.S. government deleted satellite images of it from databases. Not

CELEBRATING "THE INCIDENT"

Each year, Roswell, New Mexico, holds a UFO Festival to mark the date of the UFO event of 1947. People dress in costumes and take part in activities such as parades and contests. Scientists, authors, and other serious guest speakers talk about the possibility of alien life. Roswell is also home to the International UFO Museum and Research Center, which is open year-round to visitors.

A participant in the festivities in Roswell, New Mexico, takes some "alien" friends for a ride through downtown. UFO enthusiasts can easily find other believers in Roswell.

This is a guard gate at Area 51. Numerous security guards patrol the perimeter of the base, too. Area 51 is a testing facility for advanced aircraft as well as other secret projects.

until 2000 were photographs originating from a Soviet satellite released by an organization of scientists. These images show a base on many acres of land in Nevada, northwest of Las Vegas. There are several buildings, including hangars for aircraft. Some think that a much larger base is located underground.

According to the air force, Area 51's purpose is "the testing of technologies and systems training for operations critical to the effectiveness of U.S. military forces and the security of the United States." Workers there take an oath of secrecy. One engineer said that he was not even allowed to tell his wife where he went to work. None of the buildings in Area 51 have windows, and surrounding lands are blocked off so that curious hikers cannot get a glimpse of activities there. Perhaps because of all this concealment, some UFO conspiracy theorists have linked Area 51 to the Roswell Incident, believing that any remains of an alien craft could be well hidden at the facility. The air force denies this.

CHAPTER THREE

ALIEN INVESTIGATIONS

Following the Roswell Incident, there was an explosion of UFO sightings. In response, the United States Air Force began the government's first official study of UFOs—Project Sign—in 1948. It thoroughly examined 243 sightings. Project Sign was replaced by Project Grudge, which investigated another 244 sightings. In March 1952, the most ambitious and famous of the UFO panels, Project Blue Book, was organized by the air force.

PROJECT BLUE BOOK

Project Blue Book had three main goals: to explain all reported sightings of UFOs, to decide if UFOs posed a threat to national security, and to determine whether UFOs were equipped with advanced technology that the United States could use. The panel employed physicists, engineers, meteorologists, and an astronomer. The group examined more than twelve thousand reports of UFOs between 1952 and 1969.

In 1968, the air force asked physicist Edward Condon to head another panel on UFO activity. The committee's report, titled *Scientific Study of Unidentified Flying Objects*, covered investigations of fifty-

Respected scientist Edward Condon headed the panel that concluded no extraterrestrial spacecraft visited Earth. This decision ended the government's study of UFO sightings.

nine UFO sightings. The Condon Report, as it was nicknamed, concluded that not only was there no evidence of extraterrestrial control of UFOs, but no further UFO studies were needed. Based on its recommendations, Project Blue Book was closed in 1969 after having accumulated about eighty thousand pages of information on UFO events. Since then, the U.S. government has not had any official programs to examine UFO reports.

A few scientists publicly disagreed with the government's findings. They maintained that since a few of the most reliable UFO reports had never been explained, they could be evidence that Earth was visited by extraterrestrials.

UFOS OUTSIDE THE U.S.

Besides those in the United States, the only other official and nearly complete records of UFO sightings were maintained in Canada. Canadian reports reflected about 750 sightings and events in the late 1960s. Less complete records have been kept in Great Britain, Sweden, Denmark, Australia, and Greece. In the Soviet Union, sightings of UFOs were often prompted by secret military rocket tests. In order to hide the nature of the tests, the government sometimes encouraged the public's belief that these rockets might be extraterrestrial craft. UFO sightings in China have been similarly provoked by secretive military activity.

In 1973, a group of scientists organized the Center for UFO Studies (now the J. Allen Hynek Center for UFO Studies in Chicago, Illinois). It is one of several private groups that continue to study the phenomenon.

DEBUNKED!

According to U.S. government reports, 90 percent of all UFO sightings can be easily explained. Most of the sightings investigated turned out to be celestial objects, such as stars or bright planets such as Venus, or atmospheric events such as auroras or falling meteors. Other sightings

This famous photograph was taken in 1952 by a member of the U.S. Coast Guard. It is still not clear what the four bright objects in the sky are.

were of objects such as weather balloons, satellites, aircraft lights, or bird formations.

The reliability of witnesses is one of the main considerations in all UFO reports. Also of note is the number of witnesses, how long they saw the UFOs, how far away they were from the UFOs, and the weather conditions at the time of the sighting.

One of the most common features of UFO reports is that witnesses insist that the objects they saw were under intelligent control. People come to this conclusion

PRESIDENTIAL SIGHTINGS

Skeptics may easily dismiss the UFO sightings of people they do not know, but what about those of U.S. presidents? Future president Jimmy Carter filed a report in 1973 with the National Investigations Committee on Aerial Phenomena stating that he had seen a UFO. Carter maintained that he and several others witnessed a bright moon-sized object that changed colors. He said, "The object hovered about 30 degrees above the horizon and moved in toward the earth and away before disappearing into the distance."

Ronald Reagan, who was Carter's presidential successor, saw a UFO while on a plane in 1974. The pilot recalled, "It was a fairly steady light until it began to accelerate. Then it appeared to elongate. . . . The UFO went from a normal cruise speed to a fantastic speed instantly." Reagan said, "All of a sudden, to our utter amazement it went straight up into the heavens."

because they believe they see objects flying in formation or toward another object or changing direction or speed dramatically. People have a natural desire to understand everything they see, so visual UFO sightings are the least reliable. The human eye can be tricked to the point of hallucination. A bright light in the sky often appears to move, though a fixed telescope would show it to be unmoving. An impression of distance is also untrustworthy. Reflections from windows or eyeglasses may provide superimposed views. Optical defects can turn points of light into saucer-shaped objects.

A British man took this photo of two lights he saw "hovering" in the sky. He said he saw them for only a few seconds before they raced away at an incredible speed.

Radar sightings, while more dependable, do not provide the information necessary to discriminate between physical objects and natural phenomena such as rain, meteor trails, ionized gas, or masses of heated air. Effects such as electronic interference and reflections from a region of humidity such as a cloud can also give false radar echoes.

Even so-called contact events, such as people claiming to have been abducted by aliens, have been found most frequently to involve dreams or hallucinations. The reliability of such reports depends heavily on the presence of independent witnesses.

CARL SAGAN: EARLY SETI CHAMPION

Carl Sagan (1934–96) was an astronomer who advanced the understanding of the origin of life in Earth's earliest atmosphere. Born in Brooklyn, New York, his early work focused on the physical conditions of the planets, especially the atmospheres of Venus and Jupiter. He became interested in the search for extraterrestrial intelligence, though he was criticized by other scientists for doing so. Sagan codesigned the messages for extraterrestrial life carried by the *Pioneer* and *Voyager* space probes. He was also a popular writer and hosted the television program *Cosmos*. Among his many books is the science fiction novel *Contact*, which became a film in 1997.

Carl Sagan was a very famous scientist in America in the 1980s and 1990s for his work in many realms of science. He was open to the idea of extraterrestrial life.

THE SETI SEARCH CONTINUES

A continuing organized scientific effort called SETI (Search for Extraterrestrial Intelligence) hunts for signs of intelligent life in other parts of the universe. It began actively in 1960, when American astronomer Frank Drake searched for radio signals from two nearby stars. SETI researchers assume that any advanced civilization would produce electromagnetic signals, so they look for signal patterns that would not occur naturally. SETI searches include concentrating on groups of sun-like stars as well as systematic surveys covering all directions. SETI programs

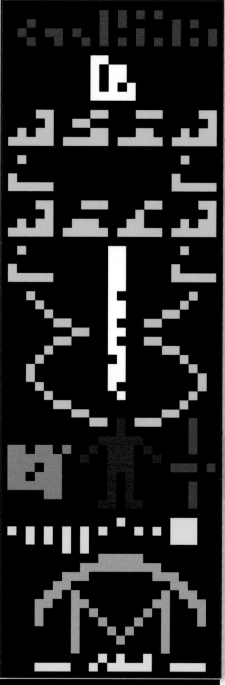

This message was beamed into space by a radio telescope in 1974. It is a seven-part message—written by Frank Drake, Carl Sagan, and others— to alien beings about life on Earth.

begun by NASA in the 1970s were terminated in 1993, forcing SETI researchers to organize privately funded projects.

The SETI Institute is a nonprofit corporation founded in 1984. Its mission is to "explore, understand, and explain the origin and nature of life in the universe." SETI scientists also work with NASA and in related industries. The institute includes the Center for SETI Research, the Carl Sagan Center for the Study of Life in the Universe, and the Center for Education and Public Outreach.

CHAPTER FOUR

ALIENS IN POPULAR CULTURE

ithout a doubt, aliens and UFOs exist and are thriving in at least one place: popular culture. Both are frequently the subjects of TV shows, movies, books, comic books, and other media. Aliens are portrayed as evil, kind, sympathetic, mischievous, funny, and, most of all, curious about the human race. In other words, they are depicted as being a lot like people. Both skeptics and believers can agree that extraterrestrials have "invaded" the entertainment industry, and they have been doing so for many years.

THE WAR OF THE WORLDS

First published in 1898, *The War of the Worlds* was a popular science fiction novel by British author H. G. Wells. Wells

A poster announces a movie released in 1950 based on H. G. Wells's wildly popular book The War of the Worlds.

spun a thrilling tale of invaders from Mars—basically brains with tentacles—brutally attacking Earth. Although it was not the first story about aliens, or even about alien invasion, it was the most popular to date, and it inspired more literature on similar topics.

There have been many adaptations of *The War of the Worlds*. Perhaps the most famous was a radio drama performed by actor Orson Welles that was first aired on October 30, 1938. People all over the United States heard a frightened radio announcer report that Martians had landed in a small town in New Jersey. Although most listeners knew that the report was part of a radio drama, thousands of panicked Americans supposedly did not, and they are said to have called the police and other authorities to find out what to do.

Wells's book has also been adapted into film several times, including 2005's *War of the Worlds*, directed by Steven Spielberg and starring Tom Cruise. It made more than $234 million, proving the draw of a storyline about an extraterrestrial menace.

MOVIES AND TV

The films *The Day the Earth Stood Still* (1951) and *Earth vs. the Flying Saucers* (1956) were famous for introducing film audiences to flying saucers. Sinister aliens feature in *Invasion of the Body Snatchers* (1956), a movie whose plot—aliens taking over the bodies of humans—has been adapted several times.

MIXING FACT AND FICTION

Many of the early science fiction books focusing on Mars and Martians used real scientists' observations and theories about the planet. In 1877, Italian astronomer Giovanni Schiaparelli described lines on the surface of Mars that he called *canali*, which means "channels" in Italian. Some thought he meant canals, though, which are artificial, not natural. If there were canals on Mars, they would have been made by extraterrestrials. American astronomer Percival Lowell was one of the people who believed in the canals. He thought that intelligent beings used them for irrigation. Martian canals were featured in H.G. Wells's *The War of the Worlds* as well as in Edgar Rice Burroughs's book *A Princess of Mars* (1917), which was made into the movie *John Carter* in 2012. Thanks to the many space probes that have visited Mars, we now know that the planet has no canals.

This is Giovanni Schiaparelli's map of Mars's canali. Despite interesting geological formations on Mars's surface, no liquid water has been found there.

The government is the enemy in the film E.T.: The Extra-Terrestrial. *However, a group of young people rescues the friendly stranded alien.*

However, *Close Encounters of the Third Kind* (1977) depicted people fighting a government cover-up in order to make contact with aliens that are benevolent.

One of the most beloved alien movies is *E.T.: The Extra-Terrestrial* (1982), in which an alien is left on Earth and befriended by a young boy. The *Men in Black* series of films imagines that aliens already inhabit Earth, though a special organization keeps them from revealing themselves.

The X-Files television show ran from 1993 to 2002. It chronicled the efforts of two FBI agents to uncover the

THE NATIONAL UFO REPORTING CENTER

The National UFO Reporting Center is a nonprofit organization located in eastern Washington State. It was founded in 1974 by a UFO investigator named Robert Gribble. The center has a twenty-four-hour telephone hotline to receive and record reports of people who believe that they have seen a UFO. These accounts are published on the center's website: http://www.nuforc.org. The organization has received "tens of thousands" of reports over the years, hundreds each month, including the account at the beginning of this volume.

truth about UFOs and aliens. The show drew upon much of the UFO and alien lore passed down over the years, and it later spawned two movies.

The *Star Trek* television series and movies take place in the future. The characters, which include aliens, travel to other worlds in spaceships and try to make peace among the many different beings in the universe. The popular *Star Wars* movies also feature an abundance of alien beings.

EYES ON THE SKIES

Popular culture storylines and images influence new gen-
erations of ufologists—the term for people who study

Yoda, a teacher and warrior, is just one of the many colorful alien beings in the Star Wars *movies.*

UFOs—and spark UFO sightings as well. The Center for UFO Studies in Chicago, Illinois, has advice for people who spot a UFO. First, call for other people to observe the UFO as credible witnesses. Second, watch carefully and take pictures of the UFO that include known surrounding objects. Remember as many details as possible

American ufologist George Van Tassel climbs a building called the Integratron near Giant Rock, California. He reportedly built it according to specifications given to him by aliens from Venus.

about the sighting and write them down immediately. Then, report the sighting.

A UFO sighting may turn out to be an optical illusion, a new kind of aircraft, or a hoax. However, like some of the cases examined by Project Blue Book, some UFO sightings simply cannot be explained by the available information. These are the phenomena that have gripped the imaginations of so many people over the years. People will have to keep watching the skies to find out if we are really alone in the universe.

GLOSSARY

ALLEGE To state as a fact, but without proof.

AURORA An event, typically occurring in the sky around polar regions, that is caused by interactions of gases and solar particles, which create patterns of colored light.

CELESTIAL Of or relating to the sky.

CHRONICLE To describe a series of events in the order they happened.

CLASSIFIED Kept secret from all but a group of authorized people in the government.

CONSPIRACY THEORY A theory that explains an event or situation as being the result of a secret plot.

DEBRIS The pieces that are left after something has been destroyed.

HALLUCINATION The perception of something (such as an image, a sound, or a smell) that seems real but does not really exist; usually caused by mental illness or the effect of a drug.

HOAX Something false passed off or accepted as genuine.

HYPOTHESIZE To offer something as a possible explanation.

INTRICACY The quality or state of being complex or having many parts.

IONIZED Changed wholly or partly into ions, which are atoms with a positive or negative electric charge.

LORE Traditional knowledge or beliefs on a subject that have been handed down by word of mouth or in the form of stories.

MICROBE An extremely small living thing that can be seen only with a microscope.

PANEL A group of people with special knowledge, skill, or experience who give advice or make decisions.

PHENOMENON Something that can be observed and studied, especially something unusual or difficult to understand or explain fully.

PLAQUE A flat, thin piece of metal or wood with writing on it that is used especially as a reminder of something.

POPULAR CULTURE Contemporary activities or products reflecting or aimed at the tastes of a large population of people, especially young people.

PROBE An unmanned spacecraft used to explore and send back information from outer space or a celestial body.

PURPORTED Claimed.

RADAR A device that sends out radio waves for finding the position and speed of a moving object.

REPRIMAND To formally criticize someone for doing something wrong.

SATELLITE A machine that is sent into space and that moves around Earth, the moon, the sun, or another planet.

SKEPTIC Someone who questions the truth of things.

SUPERIMPOSE To place or lay over or above something.

FOR FURTHER READING

Borisova, Gabrielle. *Carl Sagan*. New York, NY: Rosen Publishing, 2015.

DeMolay, Jack. *UFOs: The Roswell Incident*. New York, NY: PowerKids Press, 2007.

Halls, Kelly Milner. *Alien Investigation: Searching for the Truth About UFOs and Aliens*. Minneapolis, MN: Millbrook Press, 2012.

Kallen, Stuart A. *Aliens*. San Diego, CA: ReferencePoint Press, 2011.

Martin, Ted. *Area 51*. Minneapolis, MN: Bellwether Media, 2012.

Pipe, Jim. *Aliens*. New York, NY: Gareth Stevens Publishing, 2013.

Redfern, Nicholas. *True Stories of Space Exploration Conspiracies*. New York, NY: Rosen Publishing, 2015.

Richards, Dillon H. *Searching for UFOs*. New York, NY: Rosen Central, 2012.

Stewart, Gail B. *Area 51*. Farmington Hills, MI: Kidhaven Press, 2009.

Troupe, Thomas Kingsley. *The Legend of UFOs*. North Mankato, MN: Picture Window Books, 2012.

Walker, Kathryn. *Mysteries of UFOs*. New York, NY: Crabtree Publishing, 2009.

Webb, Stuart. *UFOs*. New York, NY: Rosen Publishing, 2013.

Whiting, Jim. *UFOs*. San Diego, CA: ReferencePoint Press, 2012.

WEBSITES

Because of the changing nature of Internet links, Rosen Publishing has developed an online list of websites related to the subject of this book. This site is updated regularly. Please use this link to access this list:

http://www.rosenlinks.com/UTP/UFO

INDEX